CHICKEN CARE FOR CLUELESS NEWBIES

A Practical Guide To Happy Hens And Stress-Free You

Adam J Walter

Chicken Care for Clueless Newbies: A Practical Guide to Happy Hens and Stress-Free You

INTRODUCTION

Ever dream of fresh eggs delivered daily by a feathered entourage? Sounds delightful, but the thought of coop chores and chicken mysteries can leave you scratching your head (and wondering if those eggs come pre-fried)! Fear not, clueless newbies! Chicken Care for Clueless Newbies is your clucking good guide to raising happy hens and living a stress-free life, feathers and all.

This book is your coop-side companion, packed with practical tips and tricks to navigate the world of backyard chickens. Forget frantic internet searches and confusing jargon; we'll decode everything from coop construction to egg-cellent recipes, ensuring your feathered friends thrive (and you don't lose your hair!).

More than just a how-to manual, Chicken Care for Clueless Newbies is your ticket to a world of joy, laughter, and heartwarming connections. You'll discover the therapeutic magic of coop care, the thrill of providing a sustainable haven for your hens, and the clucking camaraderie of joining a vibrant community of chicken enthusiasts.

So, ditch the anxieties and embrace the cluck-tastic adventure! This book is your roadmap to happy hens, stress-free you, and a lifetime of rewarding memories, filled with fresh eggs, feathered antics, and endless "aww" moments. Dive in, newbie friend, and let's get your coop dreams hatching!

Chapter 1: Coop Crusaders: Building Your Backyard Palace (with zero meltdowns)

Alright, clucking newbies, strap on your metaphorical tool belts and prepare to transform your backyard into a haven for feathered royalty! This is where we build the ultimate coop, a majestic cluck-castle worthy of your soon-to-be-worshipping hens. No more cardboard contraptions or leaky lean-tos – we're building a palace fit for queens (and kings, if you're into roosters with attitude).

1.1 From Blueprint to Cluck-in: Designing Your Dream Coop

Forget fancy blueprints and confusing lingo – we're talking chicken coops, not cathedrals! This is about creating a happy home for your feathered friends, not winning an architectural award. So, toss those intimidating PDFs and let's sketch your dream coop together!

Size it Right:

Imagine your hens strutting their stuff, flapping their wings, and having a grand ol' time. How many clucking gals are you planning to host? A couple of backyard buddies or a whole feathered entourage? Remember, happy chickens need space to spread out, scratch around, and maybe even throw a feathery tea party. So, give them room to roam – think at least 3-4 square feet per bird, and even more if they won't have outdoor space to explore.

Pick a Prime Perch:

Don't stick your coop in the shade of a grumpy oak or next to a barking dog. Find a sunny spot with good drainage, where the wind won't whistle through the walls and predators won't be peeking in. Think of it like choosing the perfect beach vacation spot – sunshine and fresh air are clucking essential!

Shape Up Your Cluck-Castle:

There are no rules when it comes to coop design! Rectangles are classic, hexagons are hip, and even A-frames can work. Just make sure it's easy to clean and access, with a sturdy door for you and plenty of ventilation for your hens. Remember, you're building a home, not a fortress, so keep it simple and functional.

Light It Up:

Chickens need sunshine to stay healthy and happy, so don't forget windows! Place them strategically to let in natural light and warmth, but not so low that your feathered friends can escape or curious predators can sneak in. Think of them as little peepholes for your hens to enjoy the backyard view.

Don't Forget the Roof!

A leaky roof is no fun for anyone, especially clucking royalty! Choose a waterproof material that can handle rain and snow, and make sure it slopes properly to avoid any feathery floods. Bonus points for a roof that allows some ventilation to keep things cool on hot summer days.

Voila! A Cluck-tastic Blueprint:

There you have it, clucking newbies! You've sketched the outline of your dream coop, a palace fit for feathered queens (and kings, if you're into that sort of thing). Remember, keep it simple, functional, and most importantly, sunny and spacious for your happy hens. In the next chapter, we'll transform this blueprint into a cluck-tastic reality, with walls, floors, and all the fixings! Get ready to unleash your inner builder, because your backyard palace awaits!

1.2 Tools of the Trade: Essential Gear for the Clueless Builder

Alright, clucking newbies, hold onto your feathers because it's time to gear up! We're not talking high-tech gadgets or robot chickens here – just good old-fashioned tools to build your backyard palace. You don't need to be a lumberjack or a master carpenter, just a willing recruit with a positive attitude and a can-do spirit. Let's assemble your arsenal!

The Saw-some Squad:

- Circular Saw: Your trusty sidekick for cutting wood planks and plywood. Think of it like a magic ruler that whispers, "Chop-chop!" Don't worry, we'll guide you through safe handling and straight cuts – no rogue branches or lopsided walls!
- Hand Saw: A handy helper for smaller jobs or tight spaces where your circular saw feels a bit like a bull in a china coop. Think precision work and nimble cuts, like crafting the perfect nesting box door.

The Hammer (and Friends) Crew:

- Hammer: Your trusty nail whisperer! Tap, tap, tap, and those walls and floors will come to life. Just remember, gentle taps for plywood, not Hulk smashes for bricks. We want a sturdy coop, not a feathered dust cloud.
- Tape Measure: Your best friend for avoiding lopsided coops and wonky windows. Think of it as your clucking ruler, ensuring everything is the right size, from floor space to roost height.

- Level: No one wants a leaning coop, not even the chickens! This little buddy keeps things straight and steady, making sure your walls don't tilt like a tipsy rooster after one too many treats.

Other Gear for the Clucking Enthusiast:

- Drill: Need to hang feeders or secure wire mesh? This whirring wonder comes in handy for those fiddly jobs.
- Screwdriver Set: Because not all screws are created equal! Having a trusty set of screwdrivers ensures you're not chasing runaway screws across the yard.
- Safety Gear: Goggles, gloves, and maybe even a dust mask – keeping yourself safe is clucking important! Protect your peepers and your lungs while you build your feathered paradise.

Remember: These are just the basics, your personal toolbox might have a few extra gadgets! Don't be afraid to get creative and use what you have. And hey, if you need a little help understanding which tool does what, the internet is your clucking best friend! Tons of tutorials and guides are out there waiting to guide your saw-wielding hand.

With your arsenal assembled and your confidence soaring, you're ready to tackle the next chapter – building your coop! Get ready to see those walls rise, windows sparkle, and roosts perch perfectly. Your feathered friends are going to cluck with delight at their new palace, and you'll be one proud chicken builder!!

1.3 Cluck and Construct: Step-by-Step Guide to Coop Assembly

Alright, clucking builders, grab your tools and dust off your hard hats – it's construction time! We'll guide you through each step, from laying the foundation like a feathered architect to framing the walls like a champion chicken carpenter. Don't worry, you don't need a degree in clucking construction – just follow our clear instructions and pictures, and your backyard palace will rise before your eyes (okay, maybe not that quickly, but soon!).

Laying the Groundwork:

- Clear the Site: Shoo away any weeds or overgrown bushes where your coop will live. Think fresh air and sunshine for your hens, not a jungle hideout!
- Level Up: Remember that wonky leaning tower of Pisa? Not the look we're going for with your coop! Use your trusty level to ensure the ground is nice and flat, so your walls don't end up like drunken sailors on a windy deck.
- Foundation Fun: Bricks, concrete blocks, even sturdy wooden posts – choose your foundation materials wisely. They need to be strong enough to hold the weight of your feathered palace and keep out any unwanted visitors (think sneaky foxes, not friendly squirrels).

Framing the Walls:

- Picture Perfect Walls: Think of your walls as giant picture frames for your happy hens. Cut your wooden studs and beams to the right size based on your blueprint (remember, we like precise cuts, not wild swings of the saw!).
- Nailed It!: Time to get your hammer hammering! Secure those studs and beams together with good ol' nails, making sure everything is nice and sturdy. Think strong walls, not wobbly fences your hens could knock over with a feather flick.
- Roof Ready: Don't let your feathered friends get rained on! Build a simple roof frame that slopes down to keep out the water and let in the sunshine. We're not talking about cathedral ceilings here, just a practical roof that keeps everyone dry and happy.

The Walls Come Alive:

- Wall Wrap: Think of it as a magic shield for your coop! This waterproof membrane goes under your chosen siding (wood, plywood, you choose!) and keeps the wind and rain at bay. No leaky coops allowed!
- Siding Sensation: Time to dress up your walls! Wood planks, plywood sheets, even repurposed materials like pallets can work (just make sure they're safe and sturdy). Nail them to the frame, creating a cozy haven for your clucking crew.
- Windows to the World: Let the sunshine in! Install windows high enough so your feathered friends can't escape but low enough for them to enjoy the backyard

view. Think fresh air and natural light, not wide-open doors for curious predators.

Flooring for Feather Fun:

- Solid Ground: Don't let your hens get their feet muddy! Choose a waterproof, easy-to-clean floor like concrete, gravel, or even sturdy wooden planks. Remember, it needs to handle scratching, dust bathing, and maybe even the occasional spilled seed.
- Bedding Bonanza: Top your floor with a nice layer of comfy bedding – straw, wood shavings, even shredded paper work wonders! Think fluffy clouds for your hens' little feet, not a concrete jungle they'll hate to walk on.

And Don't Forget the Doors!:

- Entry and Exit Points: Your coop needs a sturdy door for you to access your feathered friends easily. Think secure latch and wide enough for you to bring in feed and clean the coop without feeling like a contortionist.
- Emergency Exits: Just in case of unexpected visitors (think raccoons, not friendly mailmen), give your hens a smaller escape door at the back of the coop. They can cluck their way out to safety while you deal with the uninvited guests.

Phew! You've Built a Coop!

That wasn't so bad, was it? With your new skills and confidence, you've transformed your blueprint into a backyard palace fit for feathered royalty. Remember, take your time, follow the instructions, and don't be afraid to ask for help if you need it.

Chapter 2: Flock Feathers: Choosing Your Feathered Friends

Stepping into the world of backyard chickens can be a bit overwhelming – so many breeds, so many personalities! But fear not, clucking newbies, this chapter is your guide to choosing the perfect feathered friends for your flock. We'll explore different breeds, their characteristics, and how to match them to your lifestyle and needs.

2.1 Clucking Personalities: Breeds for Every Beginner

Picking your first feathered friends can be like choosing a new best friend – you want someone who fits your lifestyle and brings sunshine to your days! But with so many breeds clucking around, how do you choose the perfect feathered match? Don't worry, clucking newbies, this chapter is your cheat sheet to chick personalities! We'll introduce you to some beginner-friendly breeds, each with their own unique charm and quirks.

The Egg-cellent Egg-Layers:

- Rhode Island Reds: These fiery beauties are the Beyoncé of the chicken world – they're confident, active, and lay a whopping 250+ large, brown eggs a year! Think endless omelets, fluffy pancakes, and maybe even a little egg-trading with your neighbors. Just be prepared for their sassy strut and occasional squabble with other hens – these ladies like to be in charge!

- Plymouth Rocks: Imagine a calm, reliable friend who always delivers. That's a Plymouth Rock! These gentle giants come in various colors like barred, buff, and white, and they lay a steady stream of 200+ medium-brown eggs every year. They're perfect for families with young children or anyone who wants a low-maintenance, friendly flock.
- Leghorns: These sleek, athletic birds are the Usain Bolts of the chicken coop. They're not the cuddliest, but they're super productive, laying a staggering 300+ white eggs a year! Just be prepared for their curious nature – they'll peck at anything that catches their eye, including your shoelaces!

The Laid-Back Loungers:

- Wyandottes: These gentle giants are like the cuddly teddy bears of the chicken world. They're fluffy, friendly, and surprisingly quiet, making them great for small spaces or families with kids. Don't expect a mountain of eggs (around 200 per year), but their calm demeanor and fluffy feathers will melt your heart.

- Orpingtons: Picture a feathered marshmallow with a gentle soul. That's an Orpington! These fluffy giants come in various colors like buff, black, and white, and they're known for their laid-back personality and friendly nature. They're not the most prolific egg-layers (around 180 per year), but they make wonderful pets and will happily entertain you with their goofy antics.
- Cochin: These feathered dust mops are the ultimate low-maintenance friends. They're calm, quiet, and content to spend their days napping in sunbeams or dust-bathing in the coop. They're not big egg producers (around 150 per year), but their cuddly personality and adorable fluffy feathers will keep you entertained for hours.

Remember: This is just a taste of the clucking personalities out there! Do your research, and choose a breed that fits your lifestyle and brings you joy. In the next chapter, we'll help you match your needs and desires to the perfect feathered friend.

2.2 Eggs or Entourage?: Matching Your Needs to the Perfect Breed

Choosing your first flock isn't just about cute chicks and fluffy feathers. It's about finding the perfect feathered friends who complement your lifestyle and bring you joy. Before you get swept away by adorable chirps, let's take a practical approach and match your needs to the ideal breed.

Egg-ceptional Expectations:

- Egg-cellent Egg-Layers: If breakfast omelets and backyard baking are your dream, prioritize breeds like Rhode Island Reds, Leghorns, or Plymouth Rocks. These prolific layers churn out a steady stream of delicious eggs, keeping your fridge stocked and your neighbors begging for a dozen.
- Moderation is Key: Breeds like Wyandottes, Cochins, or Silkies offer a more relaxed pace, laying around 150-200 eggs per year. While not as prolific, they compensate with their calm demeanor and delightful personalities.

Space Considerations:

- Big Birds, Big Needs: Orpingtons, Brahmas, and Jersey Giants are gentle giants, but their size requires ample space. Ensure your coop and run can accommodate their roaming needs and provide them with comfortable living quarters.
- Compact Charmers: Smaller breeds like Cochins, Silkies, or Polish Chickens thrive in smaller spaces. They're perfect for urban backyards or those with limited square footage.

Climate Concerns:

- Cold-Hardy Clucking Crews: Breeds like Wyandottes, Australorps, or Rhode Island Reds can handle harsh winters with their thick feathers and resilient nature. They'll keep laying even when the temperature drops.

- Warm Weather Wonders: Breeds like Leghorns, Minorcas, or Spanish chickens prefer warmer climates. They may struggle in extreme cold and may see their egg production dip during winter months.

Noise Nuisance:

- Quiet Companions: Not everyone appreciates a dawn chorus. If noise regulations are a concern, consider breeds like Plymouth Rocks, Sussexes, or Wyandottes. These gentle giants are known for their subdued vocalizations.
- Chatty Charmers: Some breeds, like Rhode Island Reds or Leghorns, are more vocal, expressing themselves through frequent clucking and crowing. While charming, their exuberance might not be ideal for noise-sensitive neighbors.

Family Fun:

- Gentle Giants: Wyandottes, Cochins, and Silkies are renowned for their calm temperament and gentle nature. They're ideal companions for children and make wonderful additions to families with pets.
- Active Explorers: Breeds like Rhode Island Reds, Plymouth Rocks, or Leghorns are curious and energetic. They require plenty of space to explore and may not be as cuddly as some of their laid-back counterparts.

Remember: Choosing the perfect breed is a personal decision. Prioritize your needs and lifestyle, research different breeds thoroughly, and don't hesitate to seek advice from experienced chicken keepers. With careful planning and a little research, you'll find the feathered friends who bring you joy and perfectly complement your backyard haven.

2.3 Hatching Happiness: Selecting Healthy Chicks and Avoiding Rookie Mistakes

Bringing home your first flock is an exciting moment! But before you get swept away by those fluffy feathers and adorable chirps, let's ensure you're setting your feathered friends up for success. Selecting healthy chicks and avoiding common mistakes will lay the foundation for a happy and thriving flock.

Choosing Your Chick Source:

- Reputable Breeders: Opt for breeders known for responsible practices and prioritize bird health. Look for facilities with clean conditions, ample space, and healthy-looking adult hens.
- Hatcheries: Many hatcheries offer a wider variety of breeds, but prioritize those with good reputations and transparent practices. Ask about their health protocols and chick handling procedures.

Spotting Healthy Chicks:

- Active and Alert: Look for chicks who are bright-eyed, active, and chirping excitedly. They should be exploring their surroundings and readily responding to stimuli.

- Clean and Fluffy: Examine the chicks for clean feathers, free from any parasites or matting. Their eyes should be clear and bright, with no discharge.
- Steady Gait: Healthy chicks walk with a firm, balanced gait. Avoid chicks who appear weak, wobbly, or lethargic.
- Plump and Proportional: Their bodies should be round and well-proportioned, with no protruding bones or signs of dehydration.

Avoiding Rookie Mistakes:

- Quarantine Newcomers: Keep your new chicks separate from your existing flock for at least two weeks to prevent the spread of potential diseases.
- Proper Temperature: Chicks require a warm environment, especially during their first few weeks. Use heat lamps or brooders to maintain the optimal temperature range.
- Cleanliness is Key: Maintain a clean and hygienic environment for your chicks. Regularly clean their housing, feeders, and waterers to prevent the buildup of bacteria.
- Nutrition Matters: Provide your chicks with a balanced chick starter feed that meets their specific nutritional needs. Avoid giving them adult chicken feed, which can be too coarse and lack essential nutrients.
- Gentle Handling: Handle your chicks with care and gentleness. Avoid loud noises or sudden movements, and allow them to adjust to their new surroundings at their own pace.

Remember: By being a responsible and attentive chick parent, you'll set your feathered friends up for a healthy and happy life. Observe them closely, monitor their behavior, and don't hesitate to seek advice from experienced chicken keepers or consult a veterinarian if you have any concerns.

Chapter 3: Feeding Frenzy: Fueling Your Feathered Family

Now that your coop is a cluck-tastic haven and your feathered friends have settled in, it's time to focus on their most fundamental need – food! But fear not, clucking chefs, creating a delicious and balanced diet for your chickens doesn't require Michelin-star skills. We'll guide you through the essential ingredients, tasty treats, and hydration hacks to keep your hens happy, healthy, and laying like champs.

3.1 Cluck-Worthy Cuisine: Creating a Balanced Chicken Diet

Fueling your feathered friends isn't just about throwing them breadcrumbs and leftover fries! It's about creating a delicious, balanced diet that keeps their energy levels high, their feathers glossy, and those egg yolks a vibrant orange. Think of it as crafting a symphony of nutrients, and we'll be your culinary conductor, guiding you through the key ingredients for a cluck-worthy chorus of happy hens.

The Basics: Your Hen's Powerhouse Pellets

Imagine a big, beautiful bucket filled with tiny, protein-packed pellets. That's your commercial chicken feed, the foundation of your feathered family's diet. Choose high-quality feed appropriate for your hens' age and breed. Chicks need a different blend than mature hens, and laying hens require extra protein for egg production. Think of it as their daily dose of essential vitamins, minerals, and the power to strut their stuff around the coop.

Greens and Grains: Adding Variety to the Feast

Just like you wouldn't eat cereal for every meal, your hens crave variety too! Chop up some leafy greens like kale, spinach, or lettuce and mix them into their feed for a veggie-packed surprise. Leafy greens are nature's multivitamins, bursting with vitamins A, C, and K to keep your hens healthy and their eyes bright. Don't forget about the crunch factor! Scatter some scratch grains like wheat, oats, or barley on the coop floor. They'll love pecking at these tasty tidbits, satisfying their natural foraging instincts and keeping them entertained while adding extra fiber and nutrients to their diet.

Fruits and Treats: A Sweet Reward for Good Cluckers

Who says chickens can't have dessert? Treat your feathered friends to a sweet surprise with chopped apples, blueberries, or strawberries. These juicy bites are packed with antioxidants and vitamins, and they'll have your hens clucking with delight. Just remember, like any dessert, moderation is key! Too much sugar can be harmful, so keep it as an occasional treat.

Calcium and Grit: The Secret Ingredients for Strong Eggs and Happy Hens

Think of calcium as the superhero cape of your hens' eggshells. It keeps them strong and prevents those dreaded broken yolks. Offer oyster shells or calcium-rich treats to give your hens the extra calcium boost they need. And don't forget grit! These tiny pebbles help your hens grind their food and keep their digestive system running smoothly. Sprinkle some grit as a free-choice option, and watch them happily peck away at their secret digestive helpers.

Remember: A balanced diet is the key to happy, healthy hens. By providing a mix of commercial feed, fresh greens, fruits and grains, calcium, and grit, you'll create a delicious symphony of nutrients that keeps your feathered family singing and laying like champions.

3.2 Beyond the Bucket: Treats, Snacks, and Avoiding Nutritional Nasties

Who doesn't love a little extra something special? Your feathered friends are no different! But before you raid the pantry and toss them leftover pizza crusts (trust us, it's not a good idea!), let's explore the world of responsible chicken snacking. We'll show you how to add some cluck-worthy variety to their diet while avoiding nutritional nasties that might turn their happy clucking into grumpy squawks.

Treats with a Cluck:

- Yogurt Power: A dollop of plain yogurt can be a delightful probiotic treat for your hens, aiding their digestion and boosting their gut health. Just remember, moderation is key – too much dairy can upset their delicate tummies.

- Pasta Party: Cooked pasta (minus the sauce, please!) is another fun option. The starchy goodness will keep them entertained and provide some extra energy, perfect for those chilly winter days.
- Mealworm Mania: These wriggly wonders are a protein-packed treat your hens will go crazy for! They're a natural source of calcium and other essential nutrients, making them a healthy and delicious snack.

Snack Savvy:

- Kitchen Scraps with Caution: Leftover veggies and fruits can be offered in moderation, but be mindful of what's on the "no-go" list. Onions, garlic, avocados, and uncooked potato peels can be harmful, so stick to chicken-friendly options like carrots, apples, and leafy greens.
- Homemade Treats: Get creative and whip up some cluck-worthy concoctions! Scrambled eggs (sans seasoning), baked apples, or even a DIY seed cake made with oats, seeds, and fruits can be fun and healthy treats for your feathered family.

Nutritional Nasties to Nip in the Bud:

- Processed Foods: Avoid processed snacks, sugary treats, and anything with artificial ingredients. These can be harmful to your hens' health and contribute to weight gain.

- Moldy or Spoiled Food: This one's a no-brainer! Just like you wouldn't eat moldy bread, don't offer it to your hens. Spoiled food can cause digestive issues and even make them sick.
- Chocolate and Coffee: These delicious treats for us are toxic for chickens. Keep them far away from your coop to avoid any unfortunate cluck-astrophes.

Remember: Treats and snacks should be just that – occasional extras to add some variety to your hens' balanced diet. Always prioritize commercial feed, fresh greens, and other healthy options, and keep those nutritional nasties at bay. With a little planning and some creative snacking, you can keep your feathered friends happy, healthy, and clucking with delight!

3.3 Watering Wisdom: Keeping Your Hens Hydrated (without the Splashdown)

Happy hens are healthy hens, and a crucial part of their well-being is ensuring they have access to clean, fresh water at all times. But keeping your feathered friends hydrated can be messy, with overflowing drinkers and soggy runs becoming a common poultry predicament. Fear not, fellow chicken enthusiasts! This guide will equip you with the knowledge and tools to keep your hens happily hydrated without the splashdown.

Understanding Hydration Needs:

Chickens, like all living beings, require proper hydration to thrive. Their water needs vary depending on factors like age, breed, activity level, and weather conditions. Generally, laying hens require around 50ml of water per kilogram of body weight daily, while chicks need even more. Observing your hens' behavior and droppings can also provide clues about their hydration status. Lethargy, decreased egg production, and dry, dusty droppings can indicate dehydration.

Choosing the Right Drinker:

The key to mess-free hydration lies in selecting the right type of drinker. Here are some popular options:

- Automatic drinkers: These provide a constant supply of fresh water, minimizing the risk of contamination and spillage. Bell drinkers, nipple drinkers, and founts are all efficient options.
- Hanging drinkers: These elevated drinkers prevent ground contamination and wasted water.
- Bucket drinkers: Simple and affordable, but require regular refilling and cleaning.

Preventing Spills and Splashdowns:

- Place drinkers strategically: Avoid placing drinkers near feed or in high-traffic areas to minimize spills and contamination.
- Adjust water levels: Ensure the water level is appropriate for the drinker type. Overfilling can lead to unnecessary splashing.
- Monitor and clean regularly: Regularly check drinkers for leaks, blockages, and algae build-up. Clean them

thoroughly to maintain hygiene and prevent waterborne diseases.

- Provide shade and shelter: Chickens tend to drink more in hot weather. Placing drinkers in shaded areas can help reduce evaporation and encourage them to drink more.

Additional Tips:

- Offer flavored water: Adding a splash of apple cider vinegar or diluted fruit juice to the water can entice picky drinkers.
- Freeze water treats: On hot days, freeze water in ice cube trays or plastic containers to create refreshing treats for your hens.
- Consider summertime supplements: Electrolyte supplements added to the water can help replenish minerals lost through sweating in hot weather.

By following these tips and choosing the right watering solutions, you can ensure your hens stay happily hydrated and keep your coop clean and dry. Remember, a little planning and proactive maintenance can go a long way in creating a thriving and mess-free chicken paradise!

Chapter 4: Health Heroes: Keeping Your Flock Fit and Feathered

Keeping your feathery flock fit and fabulous starts with regular checkups! Think of yourself as a chicken wellness detective, ready to uncover any potential health mysteries before they hatch. Here's your guide to becoming a top-notch "Cluck-tor":

4.1 Cluck-tor Calls: Essential Chicken Checkups and Wellness Tips

Just like any superhero needs regular checkups to stay in tip-top shape, your feathered flock deserves the same! This section equips you with the essential tools and techniques to become a pro at chicken wellness, ensuring your coop stays a haven of happy clucking.

Daily Observations: Your Superpower of Awareness

Think of yourself as a chicken whisperer, attuned to the subtle changes in your feathered friends' behavior. Here's what to keep an eye on:

- Activity Level: Are your chickens bouncing around full of pep or looking a bit listless? Sudden changes in energy, like decreased interest in pecking or exploring, could signal underlying issues.

- Appetite: Is the feed bowl mysteriously untouched, or are your girls gobbling it up faster than ever? A change in appetite, either increased or decreased, can be a clue to potential health problems.
- Social Interaction: Are your chickens normally chatty and sociable, or are they keeping to themselves lately? Changes in social behavior, like avoiding other hens or looking withdrawn, can be a red flag.

Weekly Examinations: Close Encounters of the Feathery Kind

Regular checkups are your chance to get up close and personal with your feathered friends, giving you a chance to spot any physical changes:

- Comb and Wattles: These fleshy bits on your chickens' heads should be bright red and warm to the touch. A pale or shrunken comb could indicate illness, so keep an eye out for any unusual changes.
- Eyes and Beak: Healthy eyes should be clear and bright, while beaks should be smooth and free of cracks. Cloudy eyes, discharge, or overgrown beaks could all be signs of trouble.
- Legs and Feet: Give those feathery feet a gentle squeeze! They should be firm and free of any swelling, redness, or creepy crawlies like mites.

Wellness Tips: Tools for a Thriving Flock

Prevention is always better than cure, so here are some essential tips to keep your chickens healthy and happy:

- Balanced Diet: Think of yourself as a chicken chef, whipping up a delicious mix of commercial feed, fresh fruits and veggies, and some crunchy grit to aid digestion. A varied diet is key to keeping your feathered friends fueled up and feeling fabulous.
- Clean Coop: Imagine your coop as a sparkling palace for your clucking royalty! Regular cleaning and ventilation are crucial to prevent the spread of bacteria and parasites. Think fresh bedding, mucky muck removal, and plenty of airflow.
- Dust Bathing Delights: Chickens love a good dust bath! Create a designated area filled with sand or ashes for them to preen, clean their feathers, and keep pesky bugs at bay. It's like a spa day for your feathered friends!
- Stress-Free Zone: Imagine a coop filled with happy clucking and gentle chirping. Minimize stress by providing ample space for your chickens to roam, hiding spots for them to feel secure, and avoiding loud noises or sudden disruptions. A calm and peaceful coop is a happy coop!

Remember, while these tips can help keep your chickens healthy, always consult a veterinarian if you notice any concerning symptoms or your feathered friends seem unwell. By being a proactive and observant "Cluck-tor," you can ensure your backyard flock thrives for years to come!

4.2 Common Cluck-ups: Recognizing and Remedying Minor Chicken Ailments

Before you break out the chicken ambulance, let's arm you with the knowledge to handle some everyday poultry predicaments! Here's your guide to becoming a confident "Cluck-Medic" for your feathery flock:

Colds and Sniffles:

- Symptoms: Runny nose, sneezing, wheezing, coughing. Think of a tiny chicken with a bad hayfever day.
- Home Remedy: Offer warm water with a splash of apple cider vinegar, electrolyte supplements to boost recovery, and isolate sick birds to prevent spreading the sniffles. Remember, chicken TLC goes a long way!

Lice and Mites:

- Symptoms: Tiny, crawling insects causing irritation, feather loss, and scratching. Imagine your coop turned into an itchy disco for these unwelcome guests.
- Home Remedy: Dust your chickens with commercially available dust baths or sprays specifically designed for poultry. Think of it as a disco ball of doom for the creepy crawlies!

Worms:

- Symptoms: Weight loss, diarrhea, pale combs and wattles. Think of a sad, skinny chicken with an upset tummy.
- Home Remedy:For each bird, crush a few garlic cloves, skin and all, and place them inside a sock. Tie this up in the bucket of water and pour in a good dose of apple cider vinegar (the real kind, live stuff with the mom). The ACV is for healthy stomachs; the garlic is for the worms. Combining the two treatments is a wonderful idea. If there is no improvement, Consult your veterinarian for safe worming medication specifically for chickens. Remember, a vet visit is the best prescription for worm woes!

Egg Binding:

- Symptoms: Difficulty laying eggs, straining, distress. Think of a chicken struggling to deliver a particularly stubborn omelet.

Home Remedy:

- The hen could find it easier to pass the egg if she takes a warm bath and then applies lubricant—like Vaseline—just inside and around the vent.
- Put her in a remote, dark area where she can make her nest safe from other birds.
- If the hen is still not able to lay the egg and is exhibiting symptoms of distress, get immediate medical attention.This natural therapy may help with symptoms when professional assistance is not readily available, but it is not meant to be a cure or a substitute for veterinarian care. The recommendations are based on

acquired experience. Consult your veterinarian immediately. Egg binding can be serious and require professional intervention. Remember, when in doubt, call the avian expert

More Tip: For all minor ailments, providing extra warmth, electrolytes, and a stress-free environment can promote healing and keep your feathered friends comfortable. Think of it as a chicken comfort kit!

Remember: While these home remedies can help with minor cases, always consult a veterinarian if symptoms worsen, persist, or involve severe issues like difficulty breathing, bleeding, or loss of consciousness. Don't hesitate to call in the chicken health professionals for serious clucks-ups!

By mastering these clucking good tips, you can confidently handle everyday chicken ailments and keep your feathered family feeling fine and dandy.

4.3 Cluck-inardian Emergencies: When to Sound the Chicken Alarm

Sometimes, even the best chicken detectives and clucking good medics need backup. Here's how to recognize when your feathery friend needs immediate professional attention:

Call the Avian Vet Right Away if:

- Your chicken is gasping for air or coughing severely: Imagine a tiny feathered friend struggling to breathe. This is a serious emergency.
- Your chicken loses consciousness or has seizures: This could indicate anything from poisoning to neurological issues. Don't delay, call the vet!
- Your chicken experiences severe bleeding or broken bones: A broken wing or a nasty gash demands immediate professional care.
- Your chicken has green or bloody droppings: This can be a sign of internal issues that need veterinary attention.
- Your chicken suddenly dies: Losing a chicken unexpectedly is always worrisome. A vet can help determine the cause and prevent further issues.

Remember: When it comes to your chicken's health, better safe than sorry! It's always best to err on the side of caution and consult a veterinarian if you are unsure about the severity of a situation. Think of it as calling in the chicken SWAT team for critical clucks-ups.

Here are some additional signs that warrant a vet visit:

- Loss of appetite or sudden weight loss
- Dull, droopy eyes or pale combs and wattles
- Unusual lethargy or listlessness
- Limping or difficulty walking
- Abnormal discharge from eyes, beak, or vent

By being observant and knowing when to call the vet, you can be your chicken's champion and ensure they receive the timely care they need to stay healthy and happy. Remember, you're their feathered guardian angel!

Keep your veterinarian's contact information readily available and have an emergency plan in place for after-hours situations. This way, you'll be prepared to act quickly and calmly in case of a Cluck-inardian emergency.

Key Terms:

- Coop: The enclosed shelter where chickens sleep and lay eggs.
- Grit: Small stones chickens swallow to aid digestion.
- Dust bath: A shallow pit filled with sand or ashes where chickens clean their feathers and skin.
- Veterinarian: A licensed professional specializing in animal healthcare, including chickens.

Chapter 5: Sanitation Squad: Maintaining a Mess-Free Coop (It's Possible!)

Keeping your coop clean might seem like an endless battle against feathers and droppings, but fear not! This chapter equips you with the knowledge and tools to become a true "Sanitation Squad" leader, transforming your coop from a chaotic cluck-hole into a sparkling poultry paradise.

5.1 Muck My Palace? Easy Cleaning Routines for a Happy Coop

Let's face it, coop cleaning isn't exactly glamorous. But before you picture yourself knee-deep in feathers and droppings, fear not! This guide unveils simple routines that'll transform your messy cluck-hole into a sparkling poultry paradise. Remember, consistency is key!

Daily Duties: The Little Things Matter

- Spot-Cleaning: Think of it as "picking up after your feathered toddlers." Scoop fresh droppings to keep things tidy and odor-free.
- Food & Water Refresh: Replace any stale water or leftover food with fresh supplies. Think happy bellies, happy chickens!

- Bedding Check: Add a sprinkle of fresh bedding as needed to keep your feathered friends comfy and cozy.

Weekly Deep Dives: Digging In for a Sparkling Coop

- Rake & Sweep: Picture yourself as a coop janitor. Rake and sweep out all the old bedding and debris for a clean slate.
- Scrub Down Surfaces: Walls, floors, and those sometimes-neglected nesting boxes? Grab a natural disinfectant solution and give them a good scrub.
- Fresh Nesting Materials: Swap out soiled straw or wood shavings for a fluffy upgrade in their nesting haven.

Seasonal Spritz: Cleaning with the Seasons in Mind

- Spring/Summer Clean: Time for a coop makeover! Perform a thorough cleaning and consider replacing heavily soiled bedding with fresh options. Think spring cleaning, but for clucking good reasons!
- Fall/Winter Disinfect: Colder weather brings potential bacterial concerns. Give your coop a thorough disinfection to keep your feathered friends healthy and warm.

Remember: A clean coop isn't just about aesthetics, it's about their well-being! These routines are your recipe for a healthy, happy, and (dare we say?) mess-free poultry paradise.

Want to reduce cleaning frequency? Consider the deep litter method! Add new bedding on top of existing layers, letting natural decomposition handle odor and make your life easier.

Embrace these routines, become a "Cluck Cleaning Champion," and watch your coop transform from messy to marvelous!

5.2 Pest Patrol: Keeping Predators and Unwanted Bugs at Bay

Imagine a coop buzzing with happy chickens, not creepy crawlies or hungry predators. That's the dream, right? Well, fear not, fellow chicken enthusiasts! This guide equips you with the tools and tactics to turn your coop into a fortress against unwanted guests, big and small.

Predator Proofing: Fort Building for Feathered Friends

Think of your coop as a castle for your chickens. Seal any cracks or holes in the walls and roof, like plugging up a leaky moat. Remember, even a tiny gap can be an invitation for sly foxes or sneaky raccoons.

Mesh Magic: Keeping the Bad Guys Out

Windows and ventilation openings are essential, but they're also potential entry points for unwanted visitors. Don't worry, you can still have fresh air! Just cover them with sturdy wire mesh, like a knight's chainmail protecting the castle gate. This keeps out rodents, insects, and anything else that might try to sneak in for a midnight snack.

Natural Deterrents: Don't Spray, Just Sprinkle

Diatomaceous earth is a natural wonder. This fine powder acts like a tiny ninja army, dehydrating and killing crawling insects like ants and mites. Sprinkle it around the coop entrance and in cracks, creating a natural defense barrier that won't harm your feathered friends.

Chicken-Friendly Predators: Welcome the Allies

Sometimes, the best defense is a good offense. Consider welcoming guinea fowl or ducks to your flock. These natural pest control experts are like feathered ninjas, gobbling up insects and keeping your coop squeaky clean.

Remember: A clean coop is your first line of defense against pests. By incorporating these tips and keeping things tidy, you can create a haven where your chickens can strut their stuff without fear of unwanted company.

Consider installing motion-activated lights around the coop. The sudden burst of illumination can startle predators and deter them from approaching. Think of it as a disco ball for bad guys, making them want to cluck out of there!

With these pest patrol tactics, you can ensure your coop is a happy, healthy, and pest-free haven for your feathered friends. So, grab your chicken-sized bug zapper (figuratively speaking, of course!), and let the pest patrol begin!

5.3 Cluck-a-doodle-doo, No Flies for You!: Natural Odor Control Tips

No one wants a coop that smells like a poorly ventilated poultry pen. But fear not, fellow chicken enthusiasts! This guide equips you with natural, effective ways to banish those barnyard bouquets and create a coop worthy of a feathered spa.

Ventilation is Vital: Let the Fresh Air Flow

Think of your coop as a stuffy room desperately needing a window opened. Proper ventilation is key! Ensure air circulates freely to prevent moisture build-up and the funky smells that come with it. Open windows and vents, but remember to keep them secure against unwanted guests.

Bedding Basics: Choose Wisely for a Fresher Coop

Not all bedding is created equal! Opt for absorbent materials like pine shavings or straw. They trap odors like tiny feathered sponges, keeping the coop smelling fresh. Bonus points for composting the used bedding – good for your garden and the planet!

Compost Connection: Turn Waste into Garden Gold

Droppings and soiled bedding aren't just gross; they're potential odor bombs! Regularly remove them and add them to your compost pile. This keeps your coop clean and transforms waste into nutrient-rich goodness for your garden.

Herbs to the Rescue: Nature's Deodorizers

Plants are nature's air fresheners! Plant herbs like mint or lavender near the coop entrance to release pleasant scents and neutralize unpleasant ones. Think of it as a fragrant welcome mat for your feathered friends (and a fragrant goodbye to unwanted smells).

Consider adding a deep litter layer to your coop. This involves adding new bedding on top of existing layers, allowing natural decomposition to control odors and reduce cleaning frequency. Think of it as a self-cleaning coop on autopilot!

With these natural odor control tips, you can transform your coop from a smelly shack to a fragrant oasis. So, grab your gardening gloves and your herb seedlings, and let the sweet smells of success (and lavender) fill the air!

Chapter 6: Playtime Pioneers: Keeping Your Hens Entertained and Engaged

Happy hens are healthy hens, and what keeps them happy? Playtime, of course! This chapter equips you with the knowledge and inspiration to transform your coop from a simple shelter into a "Cluck-topia" of fun and engagement.

6.1 Cluck-topia: DIY Toys and Activities for a Stimulating Coop

Bored chickens are not happy chickens! Just like us, our feathered friends need mental and physical stimulation to stay healthy and entertained. But fear not, fellow chicken enthusiasts! This chapter equips you with the knowledge and inspiration to transform your coop from a simple shelter into a veritable "Cluck-topia" of fun and engagement.

Think Like a Chicken:

Imagine yourself as a tiny feathered Houdini, always looking for ways to peck, climb, and explore. Now, let's design some toys and activities that tap into these natural instincts:

- The Hanging Veggie Piñata: Suspend fruits and vegetables like apples, cabbage, or peppers from strings or nets. Watching your hens peck their way to a tasty treat is not only entertaining, but also encourages foraging and beak exercise.

- Mirror, Mirror on the Coop Wall: Hang a shatterproof mirror at chicken eye-level. Not only will they be endlessly fascinated by their reflections, but it can also stimulate their brains and provide a sense of companionship (especially for solo hens).
- Ping Pong Playground: Toss in ping pong balls or plastic bottles filled with pebbles for your feathered friends to bat around and chase. It's like a mini chicken bowling alley, promoting physical activity and keeping them entertained for hours.
- Swinging Fun for Tiny Acrobats: Hang swings or perches at different heights using sturdy branches or rope. This mini jungle gym encourages climbing, balancing, and coordination, keeping your hens fit and active.
- The Cardboard Caper: Hide treats like seeds or mealworms inside cardboard boxes with holes cut out. This "peek-a-boo" challenge sparks their natural curiosity and foraging instincts, providing mental stimulation and a rewarding treat at the end.

Remember:

- Rotate the Toys: Keep things fresh and exciting by regularly switching up the toys and activities. Your chickens are smart cookies, and they'll get bored with the same old thing.
- Cater to Individual Preferences: Observe your hens and see what toys they gravitate towards. Some might

be adventurous climbers, while others might prefer leisurely pecking at veggies. Tailor the activities to their unique personalities!

- DIY or Store-Bought: Don't be afraid to get creative with recycled materials or invest in some fun chicken toys from the store. The important thing is to provide a variety of options to keep your feathered friends happy and engaged.

With a little imagination and these clucking good ideas, you can transform your coop into a wonderland of fun and stimulation. So, put on your chicken-whisperer hat, grab your crafting tools, and get ready to create a Cluck-topia where your hens can live their best, most entertained lives!

6.2 Yard Rangers: Creating a Safe and Fun Foraging Paradise

Let your feathered friends unleash their inner explorer with a secure and enriching backyard haven! Think of it as a chicken's dream vacation, right outside their coop door. Here's how to create a "Yard Ranger" paradise:

Plant Power:

- Sprinkle seeds of herbs like oregano and thyme: Not only do these provide tasty treats, but they also act as natural pest control, keeping your hens happy and healthy. Imagine a chicken salad bar that grows itself!

- Create a "greens buffet" with lettuce, kale, and spinach: These leafy delights are packed with vitamins and minerals, perfect for boosting your hens' well-being. Think of it as a five-star salad bar for your feathered friends!

Bug Buffet:

- Designate a "bug zone" with logs, leaves, and compost piles: This natural insect playground encourages your hens' natural hunting instincts and provides them with a protein boost. Think of it as a chicken-approved safari, right in their own backyard!
- Plant flowering herbs and attract beneficial bugs: Ladybugs, butterflies, and hoverflies are natural predators of harmful insects, creating a balanced ecosystem in your yard. Think of it as a chicken-friendly pest control team!

Dust Bath Delights:

- Dig a shallow pit and fill it with sand or ashes: This essential "spa day" keeps feathers clean and healthy, prevents parasites, and even helps sharpen beaks. Think of it as a one-stop shop for happy, healthy hens!
- Add dried herbs like lavender or chamomile: The fragrance not only keeps the dust bath smelling pleasant, but also provides calming properties for your feathered friends. Think of it as aromatherapy for chickens!

Obstacle Course Adventures:

- Build simple obstacles with logs, hay bales, and branches: Think tunnels, ramps, and climbing structures. These challenges encourage exploration, physical activity, and keep your hens mentally stimulated. Think of it as a chicken ninja warrior course, right in their own backyard!
- Rotate the obstacles regularly: Keep things fresh and exciting by changing the layout of the course. This prevents boredom and encourages your hens to use their problem-solving skills. Think of it as keeping the chicken obstacle course challenging and fun!

Remember:

- Safety First: Ensure your yard is predator-proof with secure fencing and eliminate any potential hazards like poisonous plants or deep holes.
- Shade and Shelter: Provide shade for hot days and a covered shelter for rainy or windy weather. Think of it as a five-star resort for your feathered friends!
- Cleanliness is Key: Regularly remove droppings and debris from the yard to prevent the spread of diseases and parasites. Think of it as keeping the "Yard Ranger" paradise clean and healthy!

By incorporating these tips, you can create a backyard oasis where your hens can forage, explore, and live their best lives. So, grab your gardening gloves, channel your inner landscape architect, and get ready to build a "Yard Ranger" paradise that will have your chickens clucking with joy!

6.3 Dust Bath Delights: The Secret to Happy, Healthy Feathers

Imagine your chicken strutting its stuff, feathers gleaming like polished jewels. That radiant plumage isn't just for show; it's a vital part of their health and well-being. And the secret to keeping those feathers in tip-top shape? A dust bath, of course!

Think of it as a chicken spa day, rolled into one sandy, ash-filled extravaganza. But dust baths are much more than just a beauty treatment. Here's why they're essential for your feathered friends:

- Feather Frenzy: Dust helps remove dirt, parasites, and even feather mites, keeping your chickens clean and comfortable. It's like a natural feather shampoo and conditioner, all in one!
- Preening Perfection: Dust baths stimulate preening behavior, which helps distribute oils and keeps feathers waterproof and healthy. Think of it as a self-administered feather wax job!
- Beak Buffing: Dust baths provide a natural way for chickens to sharpen their beaks, keeping them strong and healthy for pecking and foraging. It's like a beak-sharpening file, right in their backyard!
- Stress Relief: Dust bathing is a calming and relaxing activity for chickens, reducing stress and promoting overall well-being. Think of it as a chicken meditation session!

Creating the Perfect Cluck-approved Bath:

- Location, Location, Location: Choose a sunny, sheltered spot away from rain and wind. Think of it as a cozy, sandy sanctuary for your feathered friends.
- Dig Your Way to Delights: Make a shallow pit large enough for several hens to enjoy. It's like a mini chicken swimming pool, filled with dust instead of water!
- Fill it with Goodness: Choose fine sand or ash, adding some dried herbs like lavender or chamomile for fragrance and pest control. Think of it as a custom-blended chicken spa mix!
- Keep it Fresh: Regularly replace the dust bath mixture to ensure hygiene and prevent build-up. It's like keeping the chicken spa clean and inviting!

Remember: A well-maintained dust bath is a vital part of your chicken's health and happiness. So, grab your shovel, mix up some sand and herbs, and watch your feathered friends roll around in pure cluck-tastic bliss! They'll thank you for it with shiny feathers, happy chirps, and a renewed zest for life.

By providing this essential "spa day," you're not just giving your chickens a treat, you're investing in their health and well-being. So, go forth, create the ultimate dust bath paradise, and witness the joy of happy, healthy, feather-tastic chickens!

Chapter 7: Training Titans: Shaping Your Hens for Fun and Function

Who says chickens can't be trained? These fluffy feathered friends are surprisingly intelligent and eager to please, making them prime candidates for some clucking good training! This chapter equips you with the knowledge and tricks to become a true "Training Titan," shaping your hens for fun and function.

7.1 Clicker Cluckers: Basic Training Techniques for Budding Chicken Whisperers

Forget feather brained! Your hens are actually brilliant little clucking Einsteins, just waiting to be trained. Enter the clicker – your secret weapon for unlocking a world of feathered fun and function. Think of it as a tiny bridge between your thoughts and your chickens' actions.

Here's the clicker-tastic formula for success:

- Action: Ask your feathered friend to do something simple, like coming towards you when called. Think of it as planting a seed of behavior.
- Click: The moment they even peck in the right direction, click that button! It's like a tiny fireworks show marking the "Aha!" moment.

- Treat: Immediately reward them with a tasty treat, like a juicy mealworm or a crunchy seed. Think of it as sweet success raining down from the chicken treat heavens!

Remember, consistency is key! Short, positive training sessions every day will help your hens learn and remember, click by click. Think of it as building a ladder of learning, one tasty treat at a time.

But how does this magic work? The click marks the exact moment you want your chicken to associate with the reward. It's like saying, "Bingo! That's exactly what I was hoping for!" in chicken language.

Here are some tips for clicker clucking success:

- Keep it short and sweet: Aim for 5-minute training sessions several times a day. Attention spans are precious, even for feathered friends!
- End on a high note: Always finish on a successful click-and-treat combo. It leaves your hens feeling happy and eager for more.
- Be patient: Learning takes time, even for the smartest chickens. Celebrate small wins and avoid getting frustrated. Think of it as a marathon, not a sprint!

With the clicker in your hand and a heart full of patience, you'll be amazed at what your hens can achieve. From coming when called to hopping onto perches like feathered acrobats, the possibilities are endless! So, grab your clicker, channel your inner chicken whisperer, and get ready to witness the clucking-good magic of positive reinforcement training!

Remember, you're not just training your hens, you're building a stronger bond and communication bridge with your feathered friends. So, click away with confidence, shower them with treats, and watch your coop transform into a haven of happy, trained, and clucking-awesome chickens!

7.2 Name Game: Building Trust and Communication with Your Feathered Friends

Forget clucking numbers, it's time to give your feathered friends the gift of a name! More than just a label, a name is a powerful tool for building trust, communication, and a deeper bond with your hens. Think of it as opening a door to a world of understanding and connection.

Why Names Matter:

- Personalization: Names make your hens feel valued and special. It shows you see them as individuals, not just a feathered flock.
- Trust Builder: Calling your hens by name creates a sense of familiarity and comfort, strengthening your bond and making them feel safe and secure.
- Communication Bridge: Names become a key element in communication. You can call them to come closer, offer treats, or even gently guide them where you need them to go.

Naming Tips for Clucking Success:

- Keep it Simple: Short, easy-to-pronounce names are best. Think "Poppy," "Honey," or "Cluck Norris" (for the feisty ones!).
- Match their Personality: Observe your hens and choose names that reflect their quirks and characteristics. Is one particularly curious? Name her "Scout." Does another love dust baths? "Sandy" might be perfect!
- Be Consistent: Use their names often, in a gentle and encouraging tone. The more you say their names, the more they'll associate them with positive interactions and feel comfortable responding.

Beyond Names:

- Mimic their Sounds: Pay attention to the unique sounds your hens make. Sometimes, incorporating these sounds into your interactions can further strengthen the connection and make them feel understood.
- Respond to their Calls: When your hens cluck or make their specific sounds, pay attention and respond! It shows you're listening and reinforces the importance of communication.

Remember: Building trust and communication takes time and consistent interaction. Be patient, shower them with affection, and speak their language (both names and clucks!). Soon, you'll be amazed at how your hens respond, come when called, and even seem to understand your every word (well, maybe not every word, but you get the idea!).

So, ditch the numbers and embrace the names! With a little effort and a lot of love, you'll unlock a world of possibilities with your feathered friends. Get ready for happy clucking conversations, strengthened bonds, and a coop filled with trust and understanding. It's all in the name of the game!

7.3 Coop Commands: Useful Tricks for a Stress-Free Flock

Let's face it, coop life can get chaotic. Feathered feet can scatter, feeding times can turn into feathery frenzies, and bedtime can be a squawking symphony. But fear not, fellow chicken enthusiasts! Enter the world of "Coop Commands," your secret weapon for transforming your coop into a haven of harmony and order.

Think of these commands as little clucking spells you cast to bring peace and structure to your feathered kingdom. Here are some handy tricks to get you started:

Bedtime Breezes:

- "Up!" for Perches Paradise: Train your hens to hop onto their cozy perches at night with the clicker method and yummy treats. This keeps them safe from predators and makes bedtime a breeze (for you and them!).
- "Lights Out!" for Sleepy Snoozes: Teach them to associate a dimmed light or soft music with bedtime. This creates a calming cue and helps them settle in for a peaceful night's sleep.

Feeding Frenzy Fix:

- "Treat Time!" for Gathering Gobblers: Train your hens to gather around a designated spot when you call "Treat Time!" This prevents squabbling and ensures everyone gets their fair share of deliciousness, no pecking order necessary!
- "Sharing is Caring!" for Peaceful Pecking: Use the clicker to reinforce gentle beak-to-beak interactions when feeding. This promotes harmony and discourages feathery food fights.

Chaos-Calming Commands:

- "Coop!" for Gathering Time: Gently guide your hens back into the coop by saying "Coop!" and offering a small treat. This makes gathering time less stressful and ensures everyone is safely tucked in.
- "Quiet Please!" for Calming Cackling: Train your hens to respond to a specific sound or gesture (like holding your hand up) when things get too loud. This can be a lifesaver during egg-laying sprees or unexpected disruptions.

Remember:

- Start Simple: Begin with basic commands and gradually increase difficulty as your hens master the basics. Think of it as climbing the coop command ladder, one click at a time!

- Positive Reinforcement: Always use positive reinforcement with treats and praise. This makes training fun and encourages your hens to learn.
- Patience is Key: Learning takes time, even for the smartest chickens. Be patient and celebrate small wins along the way.

With these "Coop Commands" in your clucking arsenal, you'll be amazed at how much smoother and more enjoyable coop life can be. So, grab your clicker, channel your inner chicken whisperer, and get ready to witness the magic of a well-trained, happy, and stress-free flock! Remember, a little communication goes a long way in creating a clucking-awesome coop where everyone feels safe, secure, and loved. Happy training!

Chapter 8: Time Cluckers: Juggling Chores with a Busy Schedule

Let's face it, between work, family, and chasing the elusive work-life balance, caring for your feathered friends can sometimes feel like chasing your own tail feathers! But fear not, fellow chicken enthusiasts! This chapter equips you with the knowledge and strategies to become a master "Time Cucker," juggling chores with a busy schedule and ensuring your hens live a life of clucking contentment.

8.1 Quick Cluckies: Daily Routines for Efficient Chicken Care

Juggling a busy life with caring for your feathered friends can feel like chasing your own tail feathers sometimes! But fear not, fellow chicken enthusiasts! Here's your crash course in becoming a Quick Clucky: a master of efficient coop care, ensuring happy hens without sacrificing precious time.

Morning Munch:

- Design a self-feeding system: Let gravity (and a bit of clever contraption) do the work! Fill a feeder with enough grub to last the day, and watch your chickens peck with glee while you sip your coffee.
- Speed-feeding station: If DIY isn't your thing, invest in a timed feeder that dispenses portions throughout the

day. No more early-bird worms stealing all the breakfast!

Water Works:

- Automatic hydration: An automatic watering system is your clucking hero! Fresh water, always available, without daily refills? Sign us up!
- Refill routine: No fancy gadgets? No problem! Simply establish a regular refill schedule, like morning and evening, to keep those beaks happily hydrated.

Eggcellent Adventures:

- Basket bonanza: Dedicate a basket near the nesting boxes for your daily egg harvest. No more playing hide-and-seek with precious breakfast!
- Egg-spiration station: Designate a cool, dry spot for storing your collected treasures. Bonus points for a cute egg carton that sparks joy every time you open it!

Spot-Cleaning Superstars:

- Poop patrol: Grab a scoop and make quick work of droppings as you see them. A clean coop is a happy coop (and nose)!
- Deep clean detours: Schedule a weekly deep clean to tackle tougher messes. Think of it as a mini coop makeover day, leaving your feathered friends with a sparkling palace.

Beak Breaks:

- Veggie volley: Toss some chopped veggies or fruits into the run for a quick foraging fun time. It's like chicken salad bowling, minus the alley!
- Treat time treasures: Hide treats around the coop and yard for your hens to discover. Watching them hunt and peck is clucking entertainment for everyone!

Remember, consistency is key! Short, daily routines like these add up to a well-cared-for flock and a stress-free you. So, channel your inner Quick Clucky, embrace the efficiency, and watch your happy hens strut their stuff!

8.2 Weekend Warriors: Deep Cleaning Sessions and Seasonal Maintenance

Think of weekends as your coop-tastic makeover days! Time to shed the feathers (figuratively, of course) and dive into some deeper cleaning and seasonal maintenance. Here's your guide to becoming a Weekend Warrior, ensuring your feathered friends live in a sparkling palace, no matter the weather.

Scrub-a-Dub-Coop:

- Glove up and get gritty! Deep clean the coop regularly, tackling caked-on dirt and disinfecting surfaces. Imagine it as a spa day for your hens, leaving them feeling refreshed and healthy.
- Bedding bonanza: Swap out old bedding for fresh, fluffy layers. Think of it as giving your hens a brand-new mattress, fit for a feathered queen (or rooster)!

- Perch patrol: Inspect perches for damage or splinters, and give them a good scrub down. Safety first, even for feathered acrobats!

Yard Rangers on Patrol:

- Give the chicken yard a once-over: Check for potential hazards like holes, loose fencing, or lurking predators. Think of it as a security sweep for your feathered fortress!
- Dust bath delight: Replenish the dust bath with fresh sand or ash. It's not just for beauty, it keeps feathers healthy and parasites at bay!
- Forage fun: Spruce up the yard with fresh greens, herbs, or even scattered seeds. Remember, happy hens are busy hens, and a little foraging goes a long way!

Coop Check Champions:

- Become a nest box detective: Inspect nest boxes for cleanliness and potential pest infestations. Fresh eggs deserve a fresh home!
- Feeder frenzy: Check feeders and waterers for cracks, leaks, or blockages. Hungry and thirsty hens are not happy campers!
- Tool time: Tighten loose screws, mend any minor damage, and give your coop a general TLC check-up. Preventive maintenance keeps things clucking smoothly!

Seasonal Savvy:

- Winter warriors: Provide extra insulation in cold weather, like deep bedding or draft-blocking measures. Happy hens deserve a cozy winter nest!
- Summer sizzle: Ensure adequate shade and cool water access during hot months. Heatstroke is no fun for anyone, feathers or not!
- Rain Rangers: Check for drainage issues and leaky spots, especially before rainy seasons. A dry coop is a healthy coop!

Remember, planning ahead makes weekend chores less daunting. Schedule your tasks, grab some music or podcasts, and turn deep cleaning into a fun, coop-tastic adventure! So, channel your inner Weekend Warrior, tackle those chores with gusto, and witness the joy of a sparkling clean, happy, and healthy coop!

8.3 Cluck-cation Station: Avoiding Burnout and Sharing the Cluck-Load

Let's face it, even the most dedicated chicken enthusiast needs a break sometimes. But that doesn't mean your feathered friends have to suffer! Here's your guide to becoming a master of "Clucking Delegation," ensuring your hens are always cared for, even when you need a well-deserved cluck-cation.

Delegate with Delight:

- Family Flock: Enlist family members in the chicken care routine. Kids can collect eggs, teenagers can refill feeders, and everyone can enjoy playtime! Think of it as a family bonding experience, feather-style.

- Neighborly Cluck-in: Ask kind neighbors to check in on your hens while you're away. A quick peek and refill can make a big difference! Bonus points for bartering fresh eggs for lawn mowing!
- Professional Poultry Pals: Consider hiring a pet sitter or chicken care service for longer vacations. Peace of mind knowing your feathered friends are in expert hands!

Vacation Cluck-in:

- Automated Awesomeness: Invest in automatic feeders and waterers for worry-free chicken care. Technology can be your clucking ally!
- Coop Cam Caper: Install a coop camera to keep an eye on your feathered friends remotely. Watching them strut their stuff while you're away is pure joy!
- Pre-Cluck Preparations: Before leaving, ensure the coop is clean, feeders are full, and waterers are functioning properly. A little planning goes a long way!

Tech-Savvy Chicken Care:

- Smart Coop Solutions: Explore automated coop cleaning robots, temperature sensors, and even light timers. Let technology do the dirty work while you relax!
- Online Communities: Join online chicken forums and groups for advice, support, and even potential co-op

care arrangements. Remember, you're not alone in the chicken-loving world!

Take a Breather:

- Don't be a Clucking Martyr! Taking breaks and prioritizing your own well-being is crucial. A happy chicken keeper means happy chickens!
- Hobbies and Heigh-ho: Schedule time for activities you enjoy, whether it's reading, hiking, or simply catching up with friends. Remember, a balanced life makes you a better chicken friend!
- Embrace the Cluck-cation: Don't feel guilty about taking a break! Think of it as recharging your batteries for even more chicken-filled adventures when you return.

Remember, taking care of your chickens should be a source of joy, not stress. By delegating, embracing technology, and prioritizing your own well-being, you can ensure your feathered friends are always cared for, even when you need a bit of "me time." So, go forth, fellow Cluck-cation Station masters, delegate with confidence, take those breaks, and return to your coop refreshed and ready to shower your hens with even more love!

Chapter 9: Troubleshooting Terrors: Conquering Common Chicken Dilemmas

Chicken troubles got you clucking your head off? Don't despair! This chapter equips you with the knowledge and strategies to tackle common chicken dilemmas, from noisy neighbors to egg-streme quirks. Remember, every feathered friend is unique, and understanding their needs is key to a happy flock.

9.1 Noisy Neighbors: Calming Cackling and Clucking Complaints

Your backyard chorus might be a symphony to your ears, but not everyone appreciates the avian opera blasting through the neighborhood. Fear not, fellow chicken enthusiasts! Here's your guide to becoming a maestro of "Coop Calming," ensuring happy hens and peaceful coexistence with your neighbors.

Location Matters:

- Coop Placement: Think strategically! Situate your coop away from property lines and bedrooms, creating a buffer zone for sound. Remember, a well-placed coop is a happy neighborhood!
- Soundproofing Solutions: Consider adding insulation or sound-absorbing materials to the coop walls. Imagine it

as a mini chicken opera house with built-in decibel dampeners!

Distraction Diversion:

- Busy Chickens, Happy Neighbors: Provide your hens with plenty of distractions like toys, herbs, or a spacious run. Think of it as keeping their minds (and beaks) occupied, leaving less time for vocal serenades.
- Schedule Adjustments: If possible, adjust feeding and playtime times to avoid peak noise hours, like early mornings or evenings. Remember, roosters don't need an alarm clock, and neither do your neighbors!

Communication is Key:

- Neighborly Chat: Talk to your neighbors! Explain your situation, listen to their concerns, and work together to find solutions that benefit everyone. Remember, a little understanding can go a long way towards harmonious backyard living!

Consider adopting quieter breeds like Silkies or Cochin chickens, known for their softer clucks and gentler disposition. Every little bit helps create a cooptastic symphony that won't ruffle any feathers!

Remember, a happy coop is a quiet coop (or at least a neighbor-friendly one!). By strategically placing your coop, providing distractions, and communicating openly, you can ensure your feathered friends can express themselves without causing a cluck-up. So, channel your inner "Coop

Calming" maestro, implement these tips, and watch the noise complaints fade away, replaced by the sweet melody of happy hens and peaceful coexistence!

9.2 Rooster Ruckus: Managing Territorial Feathered Fellas

Ah, the dawn chorus! For some, it's a charming rural serenade. For others, it's a rooster's relentless alarm clock piercing the morning peace. This chapter equips you with the knowledge and strategies to manage your rooster's territorial tendencies without sacrificing his well-being or your neighborhood's sanity.

Alternative Approaches:

- Hens Only Harmony: If rooster ownership isn't essential, consider adopting hens only. Remember, a happy hen flock doesn't require a feathered conductor to lead the orchestra.
- Confined Crowing: If keeping a rooster is your heart's desire, consider restricting his freedom during peak crowing hours, like dawn and dusk. A designated area or enclosed run can be his personal opera stage, keeping the volume down for neighbors.

Natural Solutions:

- Calming Herbs: Certain herbs like lemon balm or lavender are said to have a calming effect on roosters.

Experiment to see what works for your feathered friend, transforming him from a cluck-a-doodle-doo champion to a mellow maestro.

- Sunlight Strategies: Limit your rooster's exposure to early morning sunlight, which can trigger his crowing instinct. Consider adjusting coop placement or adding curtains to control light exposure.

Professional Help:

- Expert Advice: If you're at your wit's end, consider consulting a poultry expert or breeder. They can offer personalized advice on managing your rooster's vocal habits, ensuring he's happy and healthy while minimizing the neighborhood chorus.

Remember: Every rooster is an individual. Understanding his temperament and trying creative solutions can help you manage his crowing without resorting to drastic measures. Patience, observation, and a dash of ingenuity are key to finding the perfect harmony between your rooster's natural instincts and your neighbors' peace of mind.

Egg-streme Makeovers: Cracking the Code on Common Egg Quirks

Those precious breakfast ovals can sometimes bring unexpected challenges! But fear not, fellow chicken enthusiasts! Here's your crash course in becoming an "Egg Whisperer," tackling broken treasures, picky eaters, and other egg-streme quirks with confidence.

9.3 Broken Eggs: Don't Let Them Crack You Up!

- Frequent Collections: Gather eggs regularly to minimize breakage. Think of it as a treasure hunt for delicious surprises, before they become messy surprises!
- Nesting Box TLC: Ensure nesting boxes have soft bedding and aren't overcrowded. A comfy nest makes for a happy (and unbroken!) egg-laying experience.
- Gentle Handling: Be mindful when collecting eggs, avoiding bumps or drops. Imagine them as fragile Fabergé eggs, fit for royalty (or at least your breakfast table!).

Picky Eaters: Beyond Scrambled Shells

- Variety is the Spice of Life: Offer your hens a diverse diet of fresh fruits, vegetables, and grains. Cater to their individual preferences, just like you would with any picky eater!
- Hidden Gems: Sneak in some hidden nutrients. Blend veggies into treats or mix them with their usual feed. Remember, a little culinary creativity goes a long way!
- Calcium Cravings: If you're noticing soft eggs, consider adding a calcium supplement to their diet. Strong shells make happy hens (and happy omelets!).

Nesting Box Blues: Finding the Perfect Perch

- Think Outside the Box (Literally): Provide additional nesting options like baskets or secluded corners within the coop. Some hens just have unconventional tastes!
- Privacy Matters: Ensure nesting boxes have enough privacy and are spaced apart to avoid competition or egg-napping attempts. Remember, a happy hen lays happy eggs, and privacy plays a big role!
- Location, Location, Location: Place nesting boxes in a quiet, draft-free area of the coop. Think of it as a little egg-laying sanctuary for your feathered friends.

Bonus Tip: Keep a record of your hens' egg-laying habits. This can help you identify potential issues like nutritional deficiencies or stress factors that might be affecting their egg production.

Remember, every hen is unique with her own quirks and preferences when it comes to egg-laying. By being patient, observant, and offering a little variety and TLC, you can crack the code on these egg-streme challenges and ensure a steady flow of delicious, healthy breakfast treasures! So, channel your inner Egg Whisperer, implement these tips, and watch those egg-cellent surprises keep rolling in!

Chapter 10: Clucking Up a Community: Connecting and Sharing Your Chicken Passion

Owning chickens isn't just about fresh eggs and feathered friends; it's about connecting with a vibrant community of fellow chicken enthusiasts! This chapter equips you with the tools to become a master "Cluck Connector," finding local communities, events, and even inspiring others to embrace the joys of backyard chickens.

10.1 Local Cluckers: Finding Your Feathered Flock

Ready to connect with fellow chicken enthusiasts in your area? Welcome to the wonderful world of "chicken-munity," where sharing your passion for backyard birds can be as rewarding as those fresh eggs! This section will guide you through various channels to discover your local cluck-munity, whether you're a seasoned chicken keeper or just hatching your first coop dreams.

Flocking to the Digital Nest:

- Facebook Feathers: Social media is a treasure trove of chicken communities! Search for groups like "Backyard Chickens in [Your City]" or "Chicken Lovers of [Your County]". These virtual flocks offer a wealth of information, support, and opportunities to connect with like-minded individuals.

- Meetup Mania: Platforms like Meetup.com host local chicken-related groups that organize exciting activities like coop tours, workshops, and social gatherings. Imagine potlucks with a feathery twist and knowledge-sharing sessions led by experienced chicken keepers!
- Twitter Tweets and Chirps: Join the #chickencommunity hashtag on Twitter and connect with chicken enthusiasts from around the globe. Share your coop adventures, ask questions, and learn from others' experiences. Think of it as a constant stream of chicken-related inspiration!

Beyond the Digital Cluck:

- Poultry Show Passions: Dive into the world of local poultry shows and fairs. These events showcase amazing birds, connect you with breeders and experts, and offer a chance to mingle with fellow chicken enthusiasts. Picture it as a feathered field trip with plenty of clucking good conversations!
- Community Calendar Clutches: Don't underestimate the power of your local community calendar! Libraries, parks, and even garden centers often host chicken-related workshops, talks, or demonstrations. Keep an eye out for these clucking good events and join the in-person cluck-munity!

Remember, the key to building connections is to be proactive! Reach out to group organizers or members online or at events. Don't hesitate to introduce yourself, share your chicken stories, and ask questions. Your enthusiasm and willingness to connect will be warmly welcomed by the local cluck-munity.

By exploring these avenues, you'll be surprised at the vibrant network of chicken enthusiasts waiting to connect. So, spread your wings, embrace the spirit of community, and discover the joy of sharing your chicken passion with your local cluck-munity!

Remember: This is just a starting point. Feel free to adapt these tips to your specific location and interests. You might even stumble upon unique local events or online communities that cater to specific chicken breeds or areas of expertise. The possibilities are endless, so get out there and start clucking!

10.2 Sharing the Cluck: Spreading the Chicken Love

The joy of backyard chickens shouldn't be a solo experience! This section equips you with the tools to become a "Clucking Ambassador," inspiring others to embrace the feathery fun. Remember, the bigger the cluck-munity, the more eggscellent it gets!

Open Coop Doors:

- Host "Coop Open Days": Invite friends, neighbors, or even local media to witness your happy hens in action. Seeing firsthand the vibrant coop life, from pecking adventures to dust baths, is often the most persuasive argument for anyone considering chickens.
- Turn Your Social Media into a Coop Tour: Share your chicken adventures online! Post adorable photos, funny videos of their quirky antics, and helpful tips on coop setup, care, and delicious egg recipes. Your social media becomes a virtual coop open house, sparking interest and inspiring others to take the plunge.

Become a Local Poultry Professor:

- Speak at Garden Clubs or Community Events: Share your chicken-keeping knowledge! Offer talks on topics like choosing the right breed, coop construction, sustainable practices, or the benefits of backyard flocks. Education paves the way for understanding and acceptance, paving the path for more chicken enthusiasts.
- Offer Chick-start Mentorship: Guide those considering taking the coop-leap! Share resources, answer questions, and provide support throughout the process. Witnessing someone successfully navigate the initial jitters thanks to your guidance is incredibly rewarding.

Focus on the positive! Share the joy your chickens bring you, the sense of connection with nature they foster, and the delicious, fresh eggs you enjoy. Your enthusiasm and genuine love for your feathered friends will be contagious, making others eager to experience the same clucking good life.

Remember, becoming a Clucking Ambassador is about nurturing the existing cluck-munity and planting the seeds for its future growth. By showcasing the joys of backyard chickens, offering support and guidance, and sharing your passion openly, you become an essential part of a vibrant network that enriches lives, one coop at a time. So, spread your wings, embrace the spirit of sharing, and watch the chicken love take flight!

Remember: This is just a starting point. Get creative! Consider local partnerships with schools for educational coop tours, participate in farmers' markets to share your expertise, or even start a local chicken-keeping blog. Every action, big or small, plays a role in expanding the cluck-munity. Take the initiative, have fun, and watch the magic of shared passion unfold!

CONCLUSION

Don't Let Your Coop Dreams Gather Dust: Cluck Your Way to Success!

Congratulations, chicken enthusiast! You've reached the end of Chicken Care for Clueless Newbies, armed with a treasure trove of knowledge and inspiration for your backyard coop adventure. But the journey doesn't end here! Remember, this book is not just a bedtime read; it's a practical guide begging to be put into action.

Don't let those egg-cellent tips and heartwarming insights gather dust on your bookshelf. Open your coop doors, grab your gardening gloves, and get ready to transform your newfound knowledge into a thriving reality. Remember, happy hens and stress-free you are just a peck away!

Start small, implement the practices that resonate with you, and watch your confidence grow alongside your feathered friends. Every clean coop, every delicious omelet made with fresh eggs, and every giggle at your hens' quirky antics is a testament to your newfound mastery.

Embrace the challenges as learning opportunities, the setbacks as temporary detours, and the successes as feathers in your clucking good cap. Remember, the chicken-keeping journey is just that – a journey. Enjoy the twists and turns, celebrate the milestones, and share your triumphs (and mishaps!) with the vibrant community of chicken enthusiasts you've now joined.

So, close this book, open your coop doors, and let the fun begin! Remember, Chicken Care for Clueless Newbies is just the starting point. The rest is up to you, your creativity, and a whole lot of love for your feathered friends. Go forth, newbie chicken keeper, and make your coop dreams a clucking reality!